# Mother Teresa
## ❦ GUIDED BY LOVE ❧

# *Mother Teresa*
## GUIDED BY LOVE

By Gremlyn Bradley-Waddell

METRO BOOKS
NEW YORK

Design: Todd Bates
Editorial: Kjersti Egerdahl
Image Research: Chris Campbell
Production Coordination: Leah Finger
Product Development: Jason Astrup
Project Management: Sheila Kamuda


Metro Books
122 Fifth Avenue
New York, NY 10011

ISBN-13: 978-1-4351-1624-5
ISBN-10: 1-4351-1624-0

Printed and bound in China

10 9 8 7 6 5 4 3 2 1

# Introduction

She was, by many accounts, ordinary. Yet she was a visionary. She was mortal, but she was probably the closest thing to a saint that many in our lifetime will see. And though she was physically small, she was a giant in humanitarian terms.

Although she's been gone from this Earth for more than a decade, Mother Teresa continues to be an inspiration to people around the world. Through her words—and, of course, her actions—she taught compassion and sympathy. She focused her energies on those discarded by society: the poor, the sick, the dying. But she also made time for politicians and princesses, although her diminutive stature, well-creased face, and simple peasant dress often contrasted markedly with her surroundings. No matter. It was always those who met her who came away awestruck.

A private person who rarely spoke about her own life, Mother Teresa urged others to learn not more about her, but more about Jesus Christ and ways to serve him. In 1950, when a church official voiced interest in writing her biography, Mother Teresa declined. "My life or yours, it's still just a life," she was quoted as saying.

Yet her story is a fascinating, uplifting one. In it, a beloved father and community icon is struck down early in life, and a happy and well-to-do family is left with only the roof over their heads. A mother rises above personal misery to make a life for her children—and, against the odds, becomes a successful businesswoman. And a shy schoolgirl chooses Jesus Christ and a life of poverty over a future that could have held a home, husband, and children. Ultimately, maybe ironically, that girl would grow up to become the woman whom millions knew as "Mother."

Here is her story, albeit a brief version. That is, perhaps, the way she would have preferred it.

# 1

## The Beginning of Greatness

On a late summer day in 1910, Agnes Gonxha ("Rosebud") Bojaxhiu was born in the Balkan town of Skopje. The world would later come to know her as Mother Teresa, the embodiment of saintliness. But on that twenty-sixth day of August, it was more than enough that Agnes had become the third child of Nikola and Dranafile Bojaxhiu. The Albanian Catholic couple already had a daughter, Aga, born in 1904, and a son, Lazar, born in 1907.

Nikola, or Kole, as he was often called, was a successful businessman with a keen interest in politics, and his family enjoyed a comfortable lifestyle in Skopje, which was then part of the Ottoman Empire and is now the capital of Macedonia. Dranafile, or Drana, was devoted to her family and the parish church, the Church of the Sacred Heart, located on the same street as their large house in the quiet community. The church

and parish priests played an important part in their lives, as Catholics were a religious minority in both Serbia and Albania. Kole was good friends with at least one archbishop, and other subsequent church officials were also friendly with the family.

The Bojaxhiu home was a loving one filled with music, literature, and discussions, as well as a nightly rosary. Kole spoke several

ABOVE: A PHOTOGRAPH OF SKOPJE, BEFORE A 1960 EARTHQUAKE RUINED MANY OF THE OLD BUILDINGS.

languages, played in a brass band, and was regarded, especially by his children, as a captivating storyteller. All three children were educated—certainly not the norm for girls at that time—and their parents set high standards for them. According to biographer Anne Sebba, he told the young trio, "Never forget whose children you are and from what background you come."

Kole's business interests led him from selling medicine, to becoming involved with construction, and finally to a partnership with an Italian merchant who sold luxury goods. He eventually owned a couple of homes and frequently traveled around Europe on business. Later, he earned a seat on the city council and even helped get the town's first theater built. But this was also a time of political upheaval in the Balkans, and war was on the horizon. A fervent nationalist who supported the independence of neighboring Albania, Kole frequently entertained friends into the late evening hours. When Albania achieved independence on November 28, 1912, a number of freedom fighters celebrated at Kole's house.

The seats in the Bojaxhiu home also were frequently filled with other guests. Although the children believed for many years that the people around the dinner table were relatives or friends, they later learned that many of these dining companions were strangers in need of a meal or a roof over their heads.

Nikola and Dranafile took it upon themselves to see that the needy in the community were fed, but performed these good deeds without fanfare.

Tragedy entered all their lives when Agnes was very young. It was 1919, and Kole had traveled to Belgrade for a city council-related meeting. He'd apparently been fine when he had departed on the trip, but he was ill upon his return home. He was taken to the hospital the next morning and had emergency surgery, but he died the next day. Kole was only in his mid-forties, and his death shook the community. A large number of people turned out for his funeral; some businesses closed for the day and children were given commemorative handkerchiefs at school. To this day, mystery surrounds Kole's passing. Sebba writes that some still believe he was poisoned, possibly because of his support for Albanian nationalism.

Drana was overwhelmed with grief. Making matters worse, her husband's business partner ended his affiliation with the family. Before long, all the Bojaxhius had was the house in which they lived. Drana also received no financial support from her family, even though they were said to have owned land and properties around Serbia. Sebba writes that the young widow believed she had some right to those assets, but Drana apparently had no paperwork to prove as much and so dismissed the idea.

Instead, after a period of mourning, she set up her own sewing and embroidery business. She also managed to maintain her home and raise three children alone, and still reached out to help the less fortunate, even in the midst of her own personal crisis.

In the meantime, Agnes—who had always been an obedient, fairly serious child—had become a disciplined young woman and a good student known for her organizational skills. She enjoyed poetry and writing, and had some articles published in a local newspaper. She had many female friends and was shy around boys.

Much like her mother, Agnes was also drawn to the church. Even as a youngster, she was enthusiastic about attending morning masses with Drana. As a teen, she worked as an interpreter, translating Serbo-Croatian to Albanian for one of the archbishop's assistants, and would occasionally tutor younger students about the basic tenets of Catholicism. She enjoyed teaching and seemed to have an inherent ability. Both she (a soprano) and Aga (a contralto) were active in the Albanian Catholic Choir and also in their church's choir, where the two were known as Sacred Heart's "nightingales."

In the mid-1920s, a new Jesuit priest arrived at the local church. He established a number of youth groups, including a Christian girls' society, the Sodality of the Sisters of Mary. Father Franjo Jambrekovic also had a zeal for foreign missions. He often spoke about the important work that Croatian and Slovene missionaries were doing in Bengal and urged congregants to pray for those working abroad. Jambrekovic also shared letters written by the missionaries and distributed Catholic magazines, like *Catholic Missions*, that featured interesting articles and photos about their experiences. Agnes was enthralled by the accounts, especially those featuring India. According to Sebba, the articles told of the adventures the nuns had while living in primitive conditions, including dealing with wild creatures running through their camps. But it was more than adventure that young Agnes sought. She had an innate interest in helping others and serving her Lord, and missionary work was an ideal fit. Biographer Robert Serrou writes that Mother Teresa's brother, Lazar, shared one instance in which his younger sister's studious interest in missionary doings became obvious to many: "Once, at a church meeting when Gonxha was twelve or thirteen, our new parish priest, a Jesuit, showed a map of the world with missions indicated on it. Gonxha amazed everyone by going up to the map and explaining the activities and locations of every one of the missions."

As it turns out, Lazar's little sister, whom he called affectionately by her middle name, had felt called since age twelve to serve God. By eighteen, after thoughtful consideration and much prayer, she realized that working as a missionary nun with the poor in India was what she wanted to do with her life. She learned that joining a teaching order in Dublin— the Irish branch of the Institute of the Blessed Virgin Mary, better known as the Loreto Order or Loreto Sisters—was an almost surefire way to get stationed in India. The missionary priests' letters that Father Jambrekovic shared often spoke of the work the Loreto Sisters were doing in Bengal. She applied to the order, then told friends and family of her intentions.

The news, it seems, was not much of a revelation to Drana. She is said to have commented earlier in life that she felt her younger daughter would not be with the family for too long, either due to illness (Agnes had some health concerns as a child, including malaria, whooping cough, and a clubfoot) or because she would give her life over to God. Drana, once assured that Agnes was committed to this new direction in life, wholeheartedly encouraged and supported the teenager—in spite of the fact that Drana surely knew the sacrifices she and her daughter would have to make. Long-distance travel was not terribly common in those days, and missionaries often did not see their families again after they departed for distant lands. Agnes certainly knew this as well.

Many friends and family also were not surprised by the dark-haired, dark-eyed beauty's decision. Lazar was, however. He had been away from Skopje for several years, at school and in the army, and had recently been promoted to lieutenant in the army when he was informed of his little sister's news. He was upset by it, and he wrote her a letter in which he asked if she realized she was "burying" herself by becoming a nun. Her response was to write back, saying essentially that while Lazar might serve a king who oversaw a few million subjects, she would get to serve "the King of the whole world."

"Which one of us is right?" she asked.

Ultimately, the Loreto Order accepted Agnes's application. And so, in late September of 1928, she found herself at the Skopje railway station, surrounded by weepy well-wishers. Her mother and sister traveled with her to Zagreb, where they waited a few weeks for Agnes's traveling companion, another young woman who had been accepted into the order. And then, in mid-October, Agnes bade farewell to her mother and sister.

She never saw them again.

RIGHT: MOTHER TERESA AT THE LITTLE BROTHERS OF THE POOR MISSION IN PARIS.

# 2

## A New Calling

Agnes and her travel partner, Betika Kajnc, arrived in Paris and were interviewed at Loreto House, a hostel owned by the order. They then went on to Loreto Abbey at Rathfarnham House near Dublin. The women had several weeks' worth of lessons in English, the language that they would use in their work, and were asked to not communicate with each other in their native language.

Agnes had also taken a new name; she was now Sister Teresa. Her name honored St. Therese of Lisieux, a French Carmelite nun who focused her prayers on missionaries and died quite young. To avoid confusion with another nun's name, Agnes used the Spanish spelling of the name. Of course, this meant she was asked without fail if she was honoring the acclaimed Spanish Carmelite nun, St. Teresa of Avila. She would always quietly correct that assumption and say that she was honoring the "little" Teresa, not the "big" one.

LEFT: AN 1886 PORTRAIT OF ST. THERESE OF LISIEUX AT AGE 13, WHEN SHE WAS KNOWN SIMPLY AS THERESE MARTIN.

In December 1928, she and Betika—now known as Sister Mary Magdalene—left on a five-week voyage to India. Upon making landfall at Sri Lanka, Sister Mary Teresa of the Child Jesus was struck by the Indian flora, the crowds of scantily-clad people, and the hot climate. The next stop, Madras, also made an impression. The poverty stunned her: people were dressed in rags and living in streets and gutters. Serving Skopje's needy had not prepared her for seeing the dead and those near death sprawled by the roadside.

The women reached Calcutta in early January 1929, but were shortly thereafter dispatched to Darjeeling. Here, in this mountain resort town at the foot of the Himalayas, they fulfilled their novitiate. This two-year period of preparation for religious life consisted of training in prayer, languages (including Bengali), spirituality, their order's history, and the order's noted strength, teaching.

In May, Sister Mary Teresa became a novice and received a traditional black habit. Nearly two years later to the day, she said her first temporary vows, committing to poverty, chastity, and obedience.

While in Darjeeling, one of her assignments was teaching at the convent's elementary school. She also assisted nurses in

a medical clinic. All the while, she wrote letters about her missionary activities for the same magazines she had read as a girl back in Skopje.

Upon completing her novitiate, Sister Teresa returned to Calcutta to live at the Loreto Convent at Entally, a compound comprising several schools. She and other nuns who served

ABOVE: MOTHER TERESA ATTENDING TO THE POOR OF CALCUTTA.

 21

with her at the time have said that she was very happy at the convent, where she was viewed as a pious, hard-working woman who also had a good sense of humor. Until the mid-1940s, she taught history and geography at a high school run by a sister organization of the Loreto Order. St. Mary's High School served a diverse group of Bengali girls, who were taught by Bengali-speaking teachers in saris. Before too long, the linguistically gifted Sister Teresa earned the nickname "the Bengali Teresa."

She also started teaching at an elementary school far from the convent. It was there that she first came face-to-face with abject poverty. Bars of soap were priceless treasures to these pupils. The children were filthy, as was the classroom. Some days, she couldn't teach until she first cleaned the room herself. That act alone, according to Sebba, astonished her young charges, who were used to seeing only those in the lowest castes perform such menial labor.

Sister Teresa was taken by the poor students' pleasure in her company. Whether or not they appreciated their lessons is not known, but they were apparently thrilled to have a teacher, to have someone who cared. Soon, Sister Teresa

RIGHT: POOR AND ORPHANED CHILDREN HAVE ALWAYS HELD A SPECIAL PLACE IN MOTHER TERESA'S HEART.

began making rounds, at first by herself, to area slums, or "bustees." She couldn't give anything more than time, but that seemed enough. A sodality group at the school also took students into the poorer sections of Calcutta, including the slum of Motijhil, or "Pearl Lake," which lay just outside the walls of the convent. Sister Teresa, not surprisingly, assisted the group. A few years later, in 1937, she took her final vows and adopted a new name, Mother Teresa, upon becoming headmistress at St. Mary's.

In the meantime, World War II was on the horizon. Calcutta became an operations center for the Allies after Japanese forces occupied neighboring Burma. In 1942, the Loreto Convent was converted to a British military hospital, displacing nuns and students. St. Mary's moved to another building in Calcutta, where Mother Teresa remained for the duration of the war, unwilling to allow the disruption of the students' education, according to biographer Kathryn Spink. To compound the wartime problems, famine struck Calcutta in the early 1940s. Natural disasters had ravaged regional rice paddies, and now rice from Burma wasn't available because of the Japanese occupation. Even if the rice had been available, most modes of transport had been given over to the war effort, and there was really no way to get rice into Bengal. As prices soared, rural residents flooded the already teeming thoroughfares of Calcutta in hopes of finding food. They typically weren't successful. In the end, millions perished from starvation.

After the war, St. Mary's moved back to Entally and Mother Teresa stepped down as headmistress, although she continued performing many of the same duties. The war was over, but food was still scarce and there was widespread tension between Hindus and Muslims throughout India as the country prepared to free itself from British rule. And so it was that a different kind of horror struck Calcutta on August 16, 1946, a sweltering summer day that the Muslim League called "Direct Action Day." Violence broke out between Muslims and Hindus after negotiations on how to divide the country stalled during a meeting at the city's main park. Some five thousand people were killed after several days of bloodshed. An estimated fifteen thousand others were wounded.

Mother Teresa left the compound after the rioting to find food for her several hundred pupils. Because Direct Action Day was considered a holiday, no food had been delivered. As she walked through now-silent streets, she saw the tragic results of the rioting; bodies lay everywhere. Some soldiers happened upon her and, evidently aghast at finding a nun out by herself in such a setting, drove her back to the convent and gave her what food they had.

Traveling to a retreat just weeks after this horrendous event, her life took a dramatic turn. She later said she had heard God's voice and that He had told her to leave the convent and to aid the poor by living among them. She referred to the September 1946 experience as a "call within a call." This day would come to be known by Mother Teresa and her order as "Inspiration Day."

She informed her spiritual director, local priest Father Celeste van Exem, of her experience after the retreat. No doubt she had probably already started forming an idea of how she would go about putting this call within a call into action. But she surely also realized doing so would require leaving her beloved Loreto Convent, leaving her beloved job in teaching and—most daunting of all—asking the Catholic Church to consider founding a new order. But, once again, she saw this as God's will.

When Father van Exem relayed the idea to the archbishop of the Calcutta Diocese, the archbishop was not enthralled with Mother Teresa's proposal to live among the poor. She was told he would need a year to consider the idea. Meanwhile, she was told to remain silent on the matter and was assigned to teach in a mining town 150 miles from Calcutta.

But while she was away, the archbishop did indeed explore Mother Teresa's idea. After a year, he allowed her to ask to be released from the convent. He made a significant change, however, in her letter to the Mother General of Loreto: he replaced the word "exclaustration" with "secularization." In other words, if she were to take on this new vocation, Mother Teresa would be living outside convent walls not as a nun but as a layperson. Applying for the indent of secularization, the archbishop believed, would call for Mother Teresa to put her trust in God. Always obedient, Mother Teresa went along with the suggested wording, even though it was not what she wanted.

When the Mother General replied, granting permission for Mother Teresa to write the Vatican in Rome, she recommended that the nun request exclaustration, not secularization. Mother Teresa did just that, but again the archbishop told her to change the wording. She did as she was told, and the archbishop sent the letter to the Apostolic Nuncio in Delhi, where it was to be sent on to Rome. Mother Teresa's request was answered in the summer of 1948, when she found out she was granted a year-long indent of exclaustration—which was exactly what she had wanted. After another year, the archbishop would decide whether she should carry on her work.

As it turns out, her letter to Rome evidently never got any further than Delhi, where at least one writer has indicated that the nunciature approved the request without sending it on to the Vatican. Another writer, biographer Eileen Egan, has surmised that if the Vatican had received such a request, the exact request—not one in which the word "exclaustration" was reinserted—would have been granted.

Whatever the case, the response to Mother Teresa's request stunned the Loreto Convent. Friends and colleagues were surprised, even devastated, that she wanted to leave. Mother Teresa, however, was eager to start her new life. She bought a couple of inexpensive cotton saris with blue stripes, the traditional peasant clothing that would be her order's new habit, and Father van Exem blessed them in the convent chapel on an August day in 1948. That evening, the nearly thirty-nine-year-old nun ducked into a taxi. Firm in her belief that God would provide, she left with just a few rupees in her pocket. This departure from the convent was almost unbearable for Mother Teresa.

"To leave Loreto was my greatest sacrifice," Spink quoted her as saying, "the most difficult thing I have ever done. It was much more difficult than to leave my family and country to enter religious life. Loreto, my spiritual training, my work there, meant everything to me."

Her next step was basic medical training at a hospital run by the Medical Mission Sisters in Patna. Father van Exem thought six months' worth of training would be prudent, but after just a few weeks, Mother Teresa pleaded to return to Calcutta and start work in the slums. The sisters at the hospital assured him she was ready. She returned in December and was given a room to live in at a home for indigent senior citizens.

ABOVE: MOTHER TERESA AT THE FREE HOSPICE FOR THE DYING THAT SHE OPENED IN CALCUTTA.

Almost immediately, she began visiting the slums of Motijhil, which had been visible from the classroom windows of the Loreto Convent at Entally. In spite of her odd appearance—a tiny European woman dressed in Indian peasant garb—she was usually welcomed. One famous account of an early visit tells of her teaching street children the Bengali alphabet by using a stick to write in the mud. But, as Spink writes, "the twenty-one pupils who arrived on the first day virtually doubled on the second and increased steadily until the noise of the alphabet being repeated was a familiar sound in the muddy alleyways that divided up the row upon row of improvised hovels."

Mother Teresa was happy, but she had dark moments, too, when loneliness, exhaustion, and second-guessing her direction in life overtook her. A few months later, she opted for a location closer to the slums and found a large, sparse second-story room in a home owned by a family that let her stay free of charge. She also rented a small shack in the slums to serve as a school. Novices, mostly former students, began showing up and, by the end of 1949, she had several helpers.

She also now had her Indian citizenship. It seemed important for her to be as much like those she served as possible. In fact, she did identify with them. The homeowner who let Mother

Teresa and her charges use his top story for free recalled traveling on a tram with the nun while those around them spoke in Bengali about the "fair-skinned lady in the sari" who was likely out converting people to Christianity. "Finally," Sebba quotes Michael Gomes as saying, "she turned to them and said, gently, but in a determined voice, 'Ami Bharater Bharat Amar,' which means, 'I am Indian and India is mine.' They were dumbfounded."

When her one-year exclaustration period ended on what the archbishop considered a positive note, Mother Teresa took the next step to move forward the plan she deemed God's will. She proposed the rules for the new order she would oversee and the archbishop sent them to Rome. Six months passed, and the news came in October 1950 that the pope had approved the Order of the Missionaries of Charity.

More sisters were entering the order, and it soon became necessary to find new lodgings. Father van Exem and another priest located a home in the middle of Calcutta and the archbishop offered the sisters a loan to pay for it; the loan was to be paid off by Mother Teresa in ten years. The sisters moved in to the home during the early months of 1953, and it is still the "mother house" of the Missionaries of Charity to this day.

It seemed only fitting that now that she had secured a home for her charges, Mother Teresa would find one for the less fortunate as well. Seeing the obvious need in Calcutta for a home where the poor could die in dignity—millions were still in need, and no amount of aid seemed to stem the flow—she asked the local government for just such a place. The government granted her the use of a pilgrims' hostel attached to the Kali Temple, named in honor of the Hindu goddess of death and fertility. The rooms were scrubbed, mattresses were brought in, and the ill, the poor, and the dying now had a place of respite. The building opened in late August 1952 and was named Nirmal Hriday, or "Place of the Immaculate Heart."

Even so, not everyone in Calcutta believed Mother Teresa was pure of heart. Some thought the Sisters would convert non-Christians when they were at their most vulnerable; some Hindus didn't want Christian missionaries on temple grounds. Most of the controversy faded, though. Even the angriest opponents walked away from the temple changed after witnessing the compassion with which the nuns cared for the destitute.

"Those who came to criticize," writes Spink, "watched as the Sisters applied potassium permanganate to the maggot-ridden wounds of the dying. They learned how Mother Teresa had lifted a young Hindu priest from a pool of his own vomit and filth and brought him to be nursed and eventually to die in peace. 'We worship a Kali made of stone,' announced another priest from the adjacent temple, 'but this is the real Ma-Kali, a Kali of flesh and blood.' "

Along with the other troubles plaguing Calcutta came unwanted children. Some were the result of unplanned pregnancies, some were too ill for their parents to care for them, and some were orphans. The Missionaries of Charity opened the doors to Shishu Bhavan, or "Children's Home," in 1955.

Other accomplishments soon followed, including a variety of homes throughout India, a town for lepers (Shanti Nagar, or "The Place of Peace") in West Bengal, and a convent in Cocorote, Venezuela—the first Missionaries of Charity home outside India. Another milestone came in 1963 with the founding of the Missionary Brothers of Charity, which began with just one priest and twelve young men whose responsibility it was to help the homeless boys who came to the city seeking wealth but ended up living at the train stations. After all, men could help the poor just as well as women—even if they did it in jeans and T-shirts, not saris.

NEXT PAGE: MOTHER TERESA AND HER FELLOW NUNS OFFER HELP TO A MAN IN CALCUTTA.

# 3

## An Inspiration to the World

By the late 1950s, the Missionaries of Charity—in the requisite and recognizable blue-and-white saris—had made quite an impact on the humanitarian front in Calcutta. Mother Teresa was a tireless and efficient manager, often staying up into the early morning hours to catch up on paperwork after putting in a full day of caring for the needy. And despite her obvious reluctance to become the center of attention, she was becoming a more recognized figure in the Indian press and throughout Asia. Thanks to the occasional photo or story in magazines and newspapers, more people were beginning to hear about the hardworking, cheerful nun and her order that lived a spartan existence, relying on divine providence to help the poor. Her order's work had also gotten the attention of—and eventual support from—some rather prominent individuals. Among them were Dr. B. C. Roy, who for a

LEFT: AS HER ORDER GREW, MOTHER TERESA FOUND HERSELF MORE OFTEN IN THE PUBLIC EYE.

time served as Chief Minister of West Bengal, and, later, Prime Minister Indira Gandhi.

A few major turning points occurred for both Mother Teresa and the Missionaries of Charity in 1960. First, the year marked the end of the church's standard ten-year probationary period, which had prohibited the congregation from expanding its efforts outside the Calcutta diocese. The Sisters took their opportunity and opened many new houses across India, including in Delhi and Bombay.

That same year, Mother Teresa was invited to attend an American convention sponsored by the National Council for Catholic Women—in Las Vegas, of all places. She had not left India for decades, but she had a strong need to get out the word about poverty in all its manifestations, including spiritual poverty, which she believed the Western world suffered from the worst. And so, after heading to Las Vegas, she took on an itinerary that included speaking before audiences in Illinois and New York as well as London, Switzerland, and finally, Rome. She even undertook her first television interview with the BBC. While in Rome, she was able to reunite with her brother, Lazar, whom she'd last seen in 1924 and who was now living in exile in Italy with his wife and daughter. She also made a formal request that the Missionaries of Charity be declared a society of pontifical right. Such recognition would allow the order to establish houses around the world.

Although she'd never spoken before large crowds and English was not her native tongue, Mother Teresa had a way of connecting with people. She didn't need to use note cards to describe her heartfelt experiences of working with the poor, the dying, the suffering, and the forgotten amidst the wretched poverty of India. Although she may not have been the most polished presenter, she was passionate and powerful; people were moved by the small, straightforward woman. She never asked for funds directly, and would never allow herself or her Sisters to take part in fundraising ventures, but Mother Teresa never seemed to leave a venue empty-handed.

Just as the West was getting introduced to her, in 1962, the Indian government gave her the Padma Shri (or "Magnificent Lotus") award, which is given to an outstanding citizen who has performed exemplary service. Her superiors in the church initially were not sure she should accept the award; there was some concern about her being singled out for a recognition that might encourage vanity. Nevertheless, she was permitted to accept the honor only—as she herself wished to do—on behalf of the world's needy and those people who were striving to improve the lives of the needy. She adopted that stance from that point on when it came to receiving awards or honors. While an award or an honorary degree meant nothing to her, receiving one typically gave her a chance to speak about Jesus Christ, faith, and the work she and the Sisters were doing. Prize money could always go toward the Missionaries of Charity. Also in 1962, she was honored with the Philippines' Magsaysay Award for international understanding.

Although it took a few years, Mother Teresa's wish for pontifical recognition of her order came in 1965. This was indeed an honor, especially since this recognition often was not granted to an order for decades. Even Mother Teresa, Sebba notes, called it "the biggest miracle of all because, as a rule, Congregations are not raised to the Pontifical Order so fast; it takes most of them many years, thirty, forty years sometimes. . . . " Almost immediately, she and a handful of Sisters set up the home in Venezuela. That area was in dire need of clergy, and so the Sisters worked mainly to serve the villagers' religious needs rather than focusing exclusively on the poor. Next came a home in Sri Lanka, and, in 1968, the Pope himself asked the order to establish a home in Rome.

Then, in the late 1960s, a bit of public relations magic occurred. Malcolm Muggeridge, a British journalist with no prior knowledge of the small nun with the

 41

well-lined face, was asked to interview her for a BBC television show. He agreed, in spite of the fact that it was a last-minute assignment and Mother Teresa had a tight schedule. As it turned out, she was uncomfortable being interviewed and there was even doubt whether the finished segment—perceived initially to be a bit on the boring side—should run. The piece aired on a Sunday night, though, and the response to it was remarkable. The world-weary, professional Muggeridge and the simple, saintly Mother Teresa had an obvious chemistry. Viewers were taken with her, and with the work she and her Sisters were doing in India; they sent letters upon letters, many to Muggeridge himself, that said as much. They also mailed in donations, which, again, Mother Teresa had not solicited.

Muggeridge, who said he was dazzled by his subject from the moment he first saw her, later urged the BBC to allow him to interview her for a more in-depth documentary. Mother Teresa reluctantly agreed, and, in 1969, found herself being filmed for five days in Calcutta. Even the crew responsible for the fifty-minute black-and-white film was amazed at how well filming went on such a tight

Left: Mother Teresa at a hospice for the destitute and dying in Calcutta, in 1969.

 43

deadline (and under some challenging conditions) and how stunning the results looked.

"One particular sequence, taken in a dark, cavernous building where the Sisters bring the dying from the streets outside, was expected to be unusable because of the poor light," Muggeridge writes in *Something Beautiful for God*, the name of both the film and the resulting book by the journalist. "Actually, to the astonishment of all concerned, it came out bathed in an exquisite luminosity. Some of Mother Teresa's light had got into it."

The film was first shown in December of that year, and Mother Teresa was on her way to becoming a household name.

Incidentally, the film's title came directly from Mother Teresa herself. According to Sebba, Mother Teresa wrote the following to Muggeridge after the filmmakers left: "I can't tell you how big a sacrifice it was to accept the making of a film—but I am glad now that I did so because it has brought us all closer to God. In your own way try to make the world conscious that it is never too late to do something beautiful for God."

What's more, Sebba writes, after the film debuted, more than 130 women joined the Missionaries of Charity in 1970, bringing the society's numbers to nearly 600.

The decade proved fruitful in other ways as well. During 1971 alone, Mother Teresa would receive the Pope John XXIII Peace Prize, the Good Samaritan Award, the John F. Kennedy International Award, and the title Doctor of Humane Letters from the Catholic University of America in Washington, D.C., her first honorary doctorate. That year also marked the opening of the first Missionaries of Charity home in the United States, right in the middle of New York City's South Bronx. Additionally, after Muggeridge published *Something Beautiful for God*, he began his quest to see his much-adored subject receive the Nobel Peace Prize.

As she expanded the Missionaries of Charity, opening houses in England, Bangladesh, and Israel, Mother Teresa earned more adulation. In 1972, she was presented India's Pandit Nehru Award for International Understanding and, in 1973, the Templeton Prize for Progress in Religion, which was presented to her in London by Prince Philip.

Unfortunately, these years were also tinged with sadness for Mother Teresa. Her mother and sister had settled

 45

decades ago in Tirana, Albania, where Aga, who had never married, had gone on to work in radio and look after her widowed mother. But as Albania turned communist and essentially became a closed society, the two women could not obtain exit visas. Mother Teresa considered going to Albania at one time, but according

ABOVE: POPE PAUL VI AWARDS MOTHER TERESA THE FIRST POPE JOHN XXIII PEACE PRIZE IN VATICAN CITY, JANUARY 6, 1971.

to Spink, she was informed that although she could enter Albania, authorities could not guarantee she would be permitted to leave. Subsequently, Mother Teresa sacrificed her own wishes rather than endanger the work of her order. Drana passed away in July 1972 without having seen her younger daughter again; Aga died just over a year later, in August 1973.

In the mid-1970s, Mother Teresa's unmistakable visage became even more familiar to the world. Her likeness was put on the Ceres Medal of the United Nations Food and Agricultural Organization, and a drawing of her appeared on the cover of an issue of *Time* magazine that carried an article on "Living Saints." In 1976, her adopted homeland of India once again lauded her, this time with an honorary Doctorate of Literature from the national university, Santiniketan Visva-Bharati University. Prime Minister Indira Gandhi was by now a good friend of the nun's despite some differences of opinion (mainly regarding Gandhi's support for government-sponsored sterilization as a solution to the country's rising population), and she personally bestowed the award upon Mother Teresa. In 1977, she was once more feted, this time with an honorary Doctorate of Divinity degree from Cambridge University. Also during the 1970s, Mother Teresa created a contemplative arm for

 47

both the Missionaries of Charity Sisters and the Missionaries of Charity Brothers. These branches not only allowed sick or elderly nuns and priests to contribute to the organization by spending much of their day in prayer, they also gave those sisters or brothers a chance to partake in some work among the poor as well. The groups, however, were later integrated back into the Missionaries of Charity.

ABOVE: MOTHER TERESA AND MISSIONARIES OF CHARITY SISTERS WALK THE STREETS OF CALCUTTA.

In spite of all the honors and adulation she received, Mother Teresa endured her share of criticism, and some books and films have questioned her methods. Some detractors have decried the quality of the medical care given at her homes, the competency and efficacy of the Sisters and staff, and even Mother Teresa's apparent disinterest in keeping (or sharing) financial records. Others have been put off by her stance against abortion and her support for natural family planning. It's also been reported that Catholic Albanians were disappointed in her for not taking a stand against religious persecution in Albania. Even her ego has been fair game, with some believing she failed to properly groom a successor, even as she grew elderly and her health foundered.

Nevertheless, the accolades kept coming. But it was the one announced in October 1979 that left Calcutta ecstatic. Mother Teresa—the unassuming nun who had preferred to toil in obscurity for so long, whose feet had grown misshapen after years of wearing ill-fitting sandals, who slept in what many considered the worst room in the Mother House in Calcutta—had been awarded the prestigious Nobel Peace Prize.

Upon hearing of the honor, she of course pronounced herself "unworthy," but noted she once again would accept on behalf of the world's poor. She traveled in December to Oslo, Norway, to accept the gold medal and make an acceptance speech. Her brother Lazar and his daughter were on hand for the festivities, as were numerous dignitaries and politicians. The prize money—about $190,000—was already earmarked to build homes for lepers and the homeless, and Norwegian youths raised tens of thousands more dollars for her charity. Mother Teresa declined the traditional banquet dinner and requested that the money that would have been spent on such a lavish meal be given to the needy. And, in spite of the political uproar it could have caused, she freely shared her unyielding view on abortion during her acceptance speech, calling the process "the greatest destroyer of peace today." The speech did create waves, yet at the same time the heartfelt words were hardly surprising, considering the source.

As the chief minister of West Bengal was said to have remarked to Mother Teresa upon learning she was to receive this great honor, "You have been the Mother of Bengal; now you are the Mother of the World."

LEFT: THE CHAIRMAN OF THE NORWEGIAN NOBEL COMMITTEE, JOHN SANNESS, AWARDS THE NOBEL PEACE PRIZE TO MOTHER TERESA IN OSLO, DECEMBER 10, 1979.

# 4

# A Living
# Saint's Legacy

In spite of her age—she was then in her seventies—Mother Teresa didn't rest on her laurels after winning the Nobel Peace Prize in 1979. Instead, she continued working at a pace that would have tired anyone half her age, traveling frequently and spreading her work throughout the world.

In 1980, she addressed the attendees at the World Synod of Bishops in Rome, and opened fourteen homes around the world. The following year, she faced personal challenges when she was diagnosed with a heart condition during a trip to the United States, and when her brother died of cancer that July. But she also opened another eighteen homes, received an honorary degree from Catholic University in Rome, and was awarded India's highest honor, Bharat Ratna (the "Jewel of India").

LEFT: POPE JOHN PAUL II MAKES A HISTORIC VISIT TO CALCUTTA IN 1986 AND MEETS WITH MOTHER TERESA.

 53

If there was any question whether she was slowing down, her actions spoke volumes. Sent in 1982 to Beirut by Pope John Paul II to let war victims there know that they were not forgotten, Mother Teresa entered the western part of the city one evening after praying for a cease-fire. The shelling was said to have stopped as she made her way to a mental hospital that had been fired on for days by Israeli troops. There, she managed to rescue more than thirty-five Muslim youths who had been left behind in all the violence and confusion. The young people, all with various handicaps, were scared and hungry. After she comforted them, she saw to it that they made it safely to a convent in the eastern half of the city. Just days later, she repeated the feat, this time rescuing more than twenty-five young people. In her biography of Mother Teresa, Spink writes about the reaction of a Red Cross official who had seen the seventy-two-year-old nun in action. He was "astonished at the efficiency and energy which went hand in hand with her spirituality. She was, he said, 'a cross between a military commander and St. Francis.' "

In 1983, Mother Teresa injured her foot after falling out of bed while in her order's Rome convent. She was encouraged to take to her bed for rest—the first time off she had taken. Then the news came from medical staff that she was on the verge of having a heart attack, which was only discovered because of her fall. Spink writes that Mother Teresa was convinced that her guardian angel had pushed her out of the bed. Of course, even these setbacks didn't keep her down for long. She often managed to be in the thick of things, whether it was meeting charity-minded rock singer Bob Geldof in 1984 or comforting survivors and the relatives of victims during a poison-gas disaster that same year in Bhopal, India.

Throughout the mid-1980s, she focused on a new problem that was gaining attention: AIDS. In 1985, she heard about the disease and went to visit patients in a U.S. hospital. She declared AIDS "the leprosy of the West," and by Christmas she was attending the opening of the Missionaries of Charity home known as Gift of Love, a Greenwich Village hospice serving men afflicted with AIDS. A second hospice opened a year later in Washington, D.C., despite neighbors' initial objections.

In 1986, Mother Teresa had what she would refer to as "the happiest day of my life." Pope John Paul II, on a trip to

Next page: UN Secretary-General Kofi Annan meets with Mother Teresa in the Bronx, New York.

 55

India, visited her at the Home for the Dying. Together, the two spoke with and helped feed Calcutta's neediest souls.

In the early 1990s, Mother Teresa met a fervent admirer who needed no introduction: Diana, Princess of Wales. The two women struck up a friendship, bonded by their goal of helping the less fortunate. Mother Teresa, according to Sebba, was later quoted as saying that Diana "is like a daughter to me."

During these busy years, Mother Teresa's health problems began to mount. Around 1990, she apparently made a request to the Vatican that she be allowed to retire. But instead, the Missionaries of Charity held an election and reelected their longtime leader. After a deadlocked election in 1997, the Sisters appealed to the pope to assist them in naming a successor. He in turn selected Sister Nirmala, a longtime Missionaries of Charity Sister who nevertheless declined to take the title of "Mother." Even though she was in a fragile state, Mother Teresa remained active. She traveled to the United States, where she received the Congressional Gold Medal, and then went back to India to celebrate her eighty-seventh birthday.

LEFT: MOTHER TERESA AND DIANA, PRINCESS OF WALES, AFTER A MEETING IN THE MISSIONARIES OF CHARITY RESIDENCE IN THE BRONX, NEW YORK CITY.

Just a few days afterward, on August 31, 1997, Princess Diana died in a tragic automobile accident in Paris. Mother Teresa planned to attend a nighttime service for the princess on September 5, but she never made it. After experiencing chest pain, Mother Teresa suffered a fatal heart attack that night. Eight days later, mourners lined the streets of Calcutta to see their "Mother" one last time as her body was borne atop the same gun carriage that had carried the bodies of Mahatma Gandhi and Jawaharlal Nehru. After a state funeral, Mother Teresa was buried in the Mother House, where her tomb has served as a place of pilgrimage for countless people. She was beatified in 2003 and now has only one step left—canonization—before she achieves sainthood.

Mother Teresa left behind several thousand Sisters, hundreds of Brothers, and numerous others associated with the Missionaries of Charity, among them volunteer coworkers, Fathers, and lay missionaries.

But perhaps the most significant things she left behind were her simple belief that people should take care of each other and her ability to do just that.

RIGHT: MOTHER TERESA GREETED CHILDREN, FOLLOWERS, AND CROWDS WITH THE SAME SMILE.

# About the Author

Gremlyn Bradley-Waddell is a writer who specializes in personality profiles. A graduate of Arizona State University, she worked as a newspaper reporter in Prescott and Scottsdale, Arizona, before turning to magazine and book publishing. She resides in Tempe, Arizona, with her husband and their three children.

# Acknowledgments

For my dear husband, Lane, who understands that his wife's place is in her home office, and for our three children—Clare London, Cameron Forrest, and Caroline Angelica—who inspire me every day.

Untold thanks also to my mom, Sharon Bradley, for her love and her love of books, not to mention her high tolerance threshold. I also thank my dad, the late author and book collector Van Allen Bradley, whose love for writing is now hardwired into my soul as well.

Bless you all.

*Gremlyn Bradley-Waddell*
*Tempe, Arizona*
*2008*

# List of Sources

I'd like to acknowledge the following books, which all proved invaluable in my research efforts:

Porter, David. *Mother Teresa: The Early Years*. Grand Rapids, MI: William B. Eerdmans Publishing Company, 1986.

Rai, Raghu and Navin Chawla. *Mother Teresa: Faith and Compassion—The Life and Work of Mother Teresa*. Rockport, MA: Element Books, 1996.

Serrou, Robert. *Teresa of Calcutta*. New York: McGraw-Hill Book Company, 1980.

Spink, Kathryn. *Mother Teresa*. San Francisco: HarperSanFrancisco, 1997.

Kolodiejchuk, Brian, MC, ed. *Mother Teresa: Come Be My Light, The Private Writings of the "Saint of Calcutta."* New York: Doubleday, 2007.

Sebba, Anne. *Mother Teresa: Beyond the Image*. New York: Doubleday, 1998.

Crimp, Susan. *Touched by a Saint: Personal Encounters with Mother Teresa*. Notre Dame, IN: Sorin Books, 2000.

Tully, Mark. *Mother*. Hong Kong: FormAsia Books Limited, 1992.

Allegri, Renzo. *Teresa of the Poor: The Story of Her Life*. Ann Arbor, MI: Servant Publications, 1996.

Muggeridge, Malcolm. *Something Beautiful for God*. New York: Harper & Row Publishers, 1971.

Chawla, Navin. *Mother Teresa*. Rockport, MA: Element Books, 1996.

# Image Credits

Every effort has been made to trace copyright holders. If any unintended omissions have been made, becker&mayer! would be pleased to add appropriate acknowledgments in future editions.

Front cover: Tim Graham/Getty Images

Page 8: Keystone Features/Getty Images

Page 10: Unknown

Page 16: Keystone/Getty Images

Page 18: Hulton Archive/Getty Images

Page 21: Nik Wheeler/Sygma/Corbis

Page 23: Kapoor Baldev/Sygma/CORBIS

Page 29: J.P. Laffont/Sygma/Corbis

Pages 34–35: AP Photos

Page 36: Bettmann/CORBIS

Page 38: Matthew Polak/Sygma/Corbis

Page 42: Terry Fincher/Hulton Archive/Getty Images

Page 46: Popperfoto/Getty Images

Page 48: Kapoor Baldev/Sygma/CORBIS

Page 50: Keystone/Getty Images

Page 52: Francois Lochon/Getty Images

Pages 56–57: Rick Maiman/Sygma/Corbis

Page 58: Mike Segar/Reuters/Corbis

Page 61: Reuters/Corbis

Image on ceramic card stand: Joe Bangay/Express/Getty Images